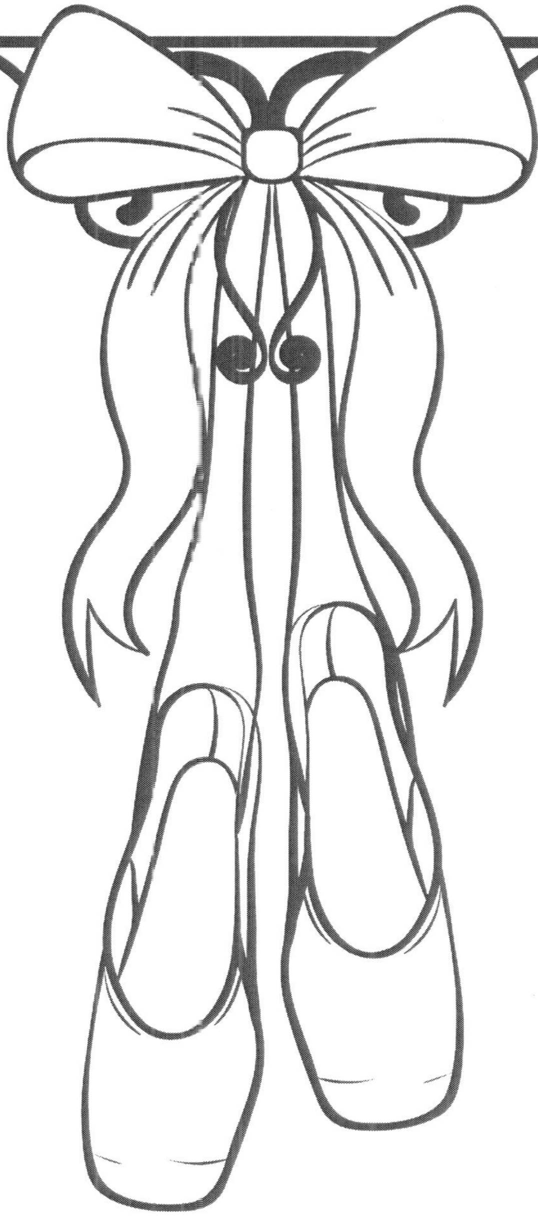

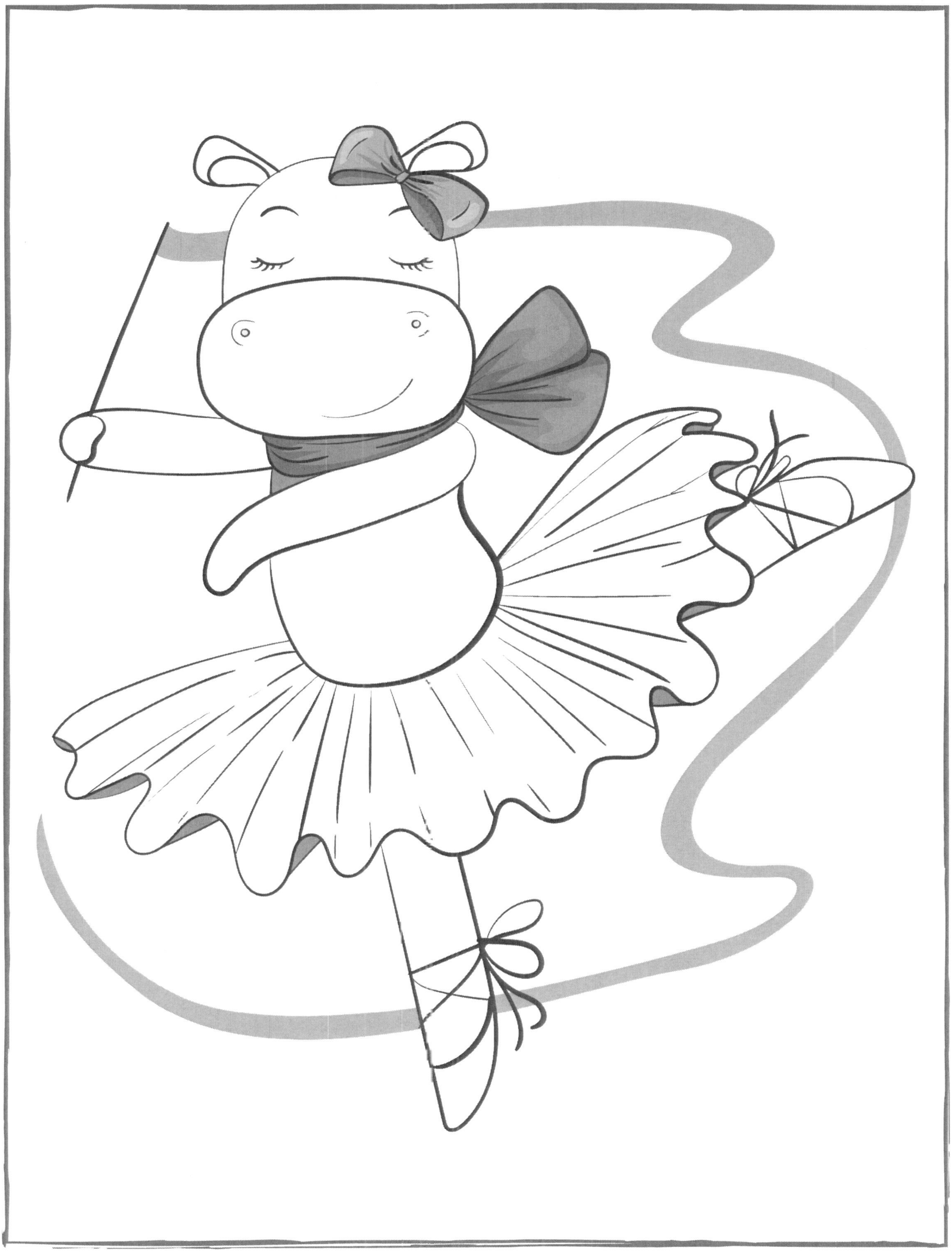

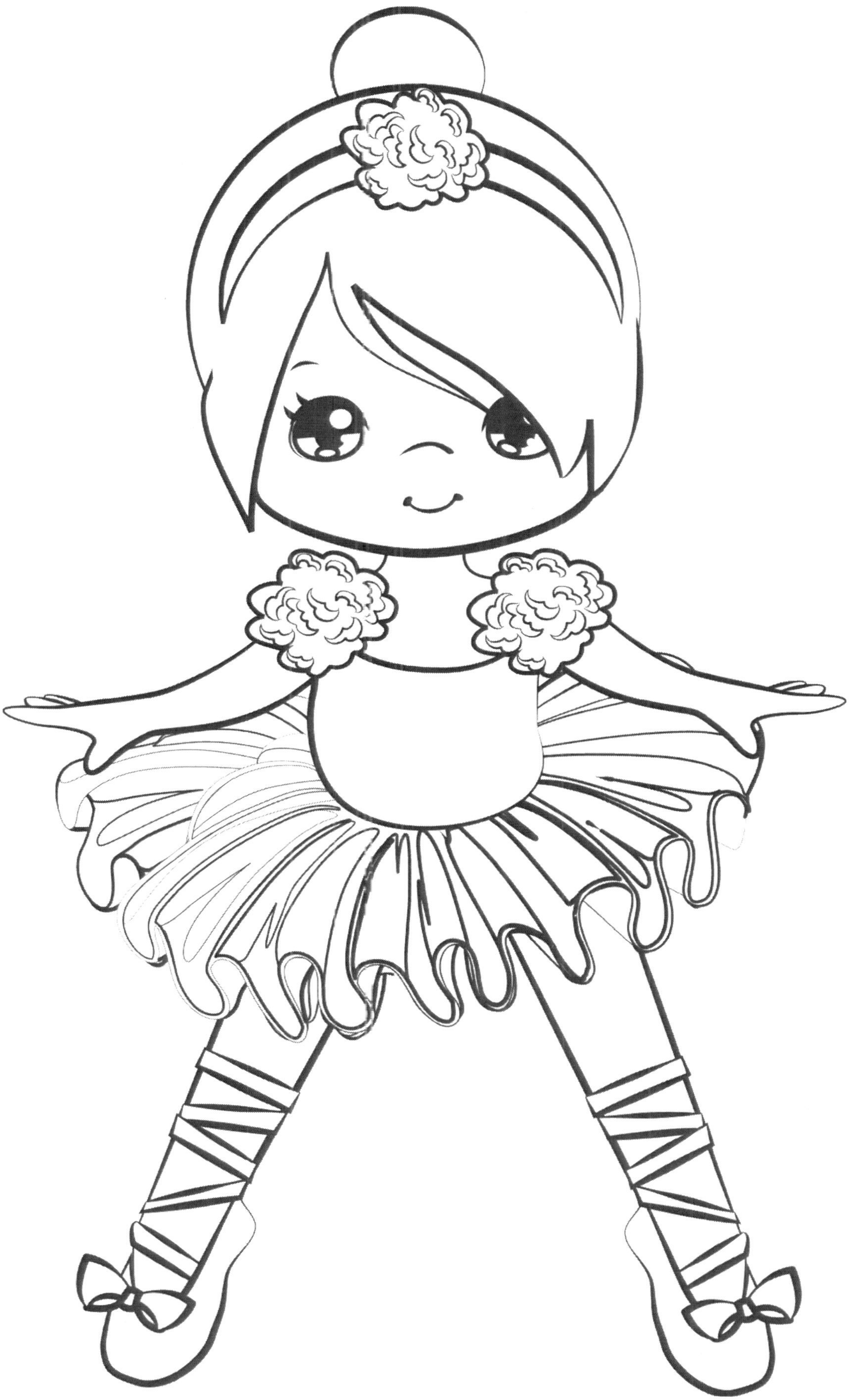

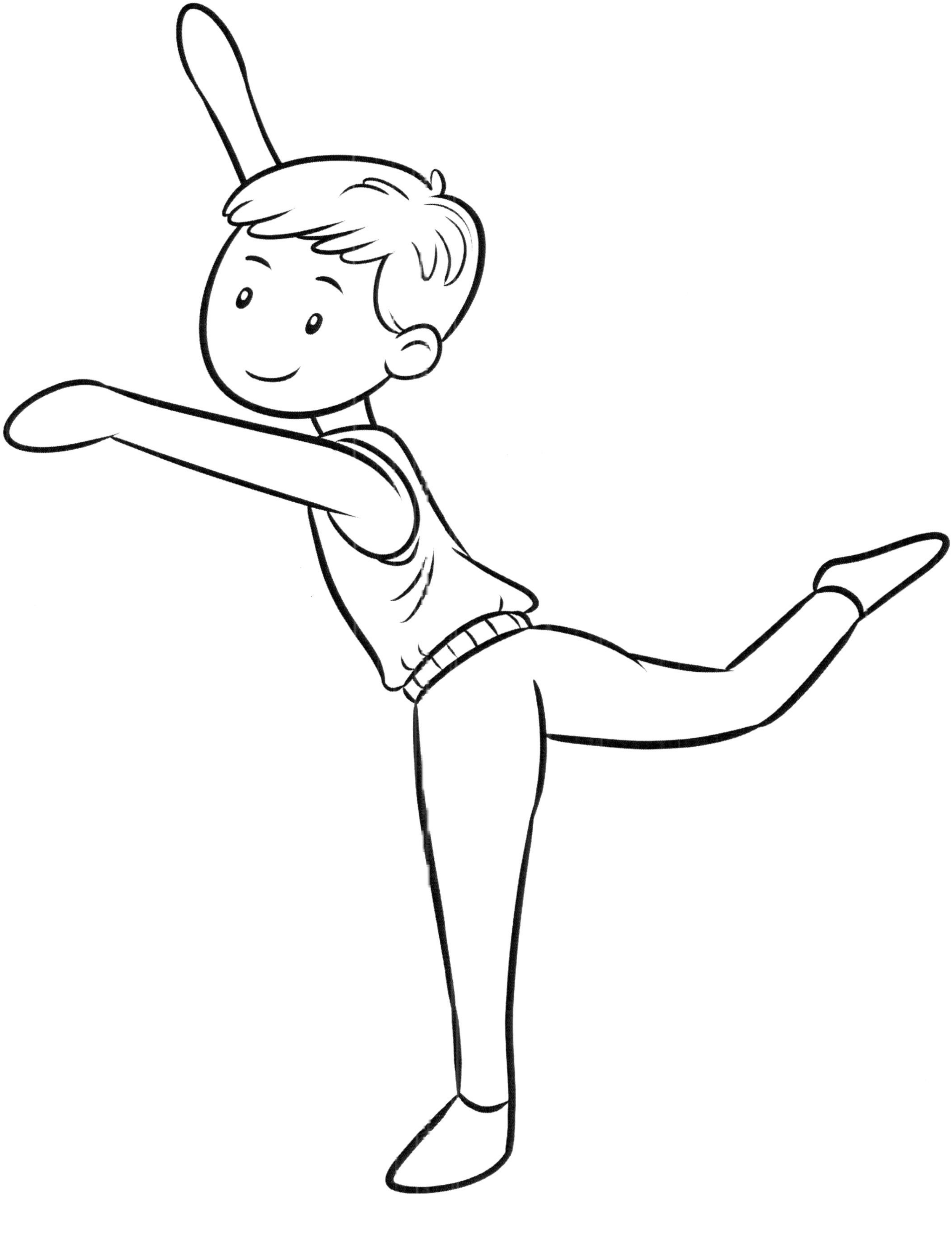

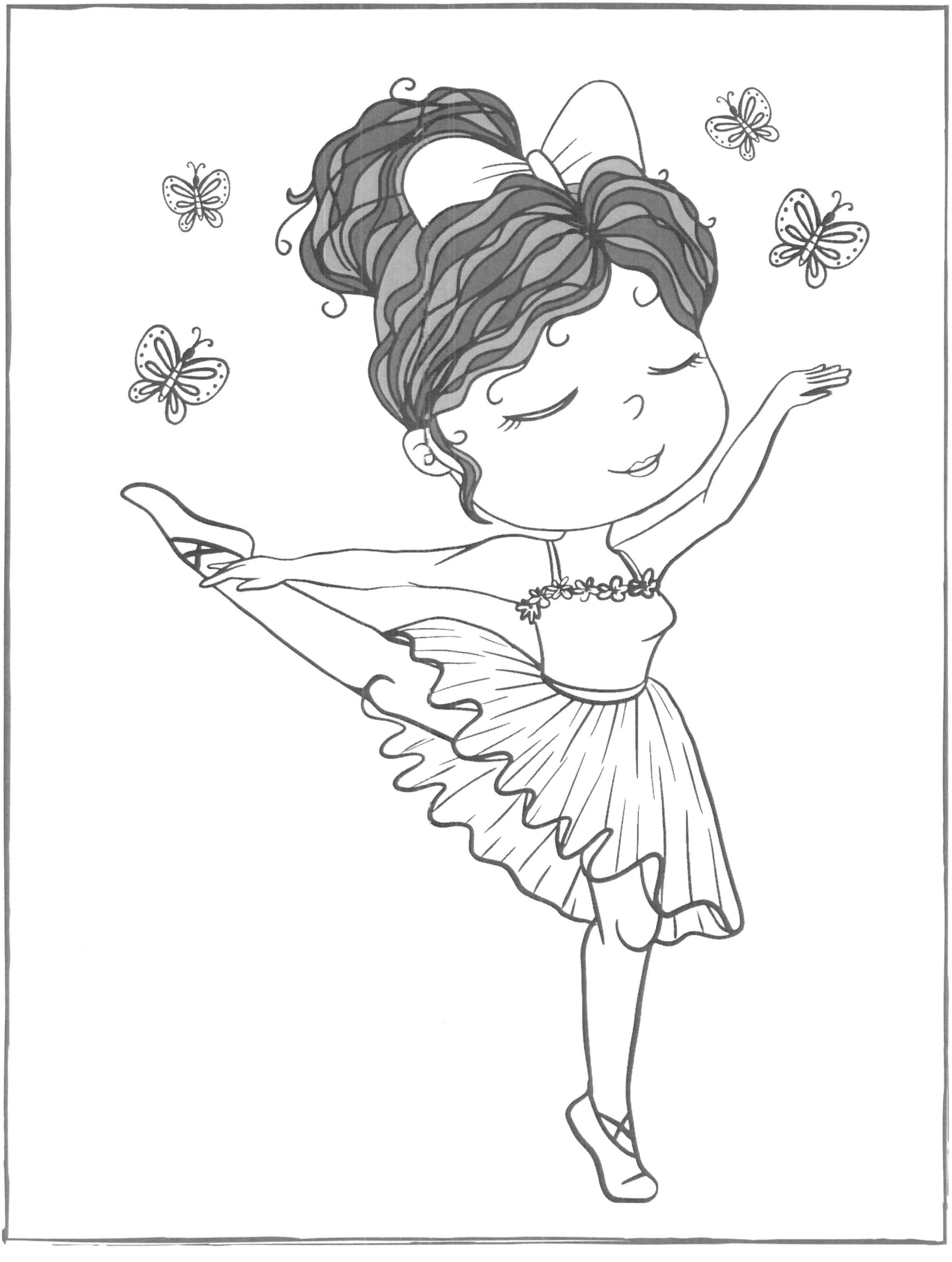

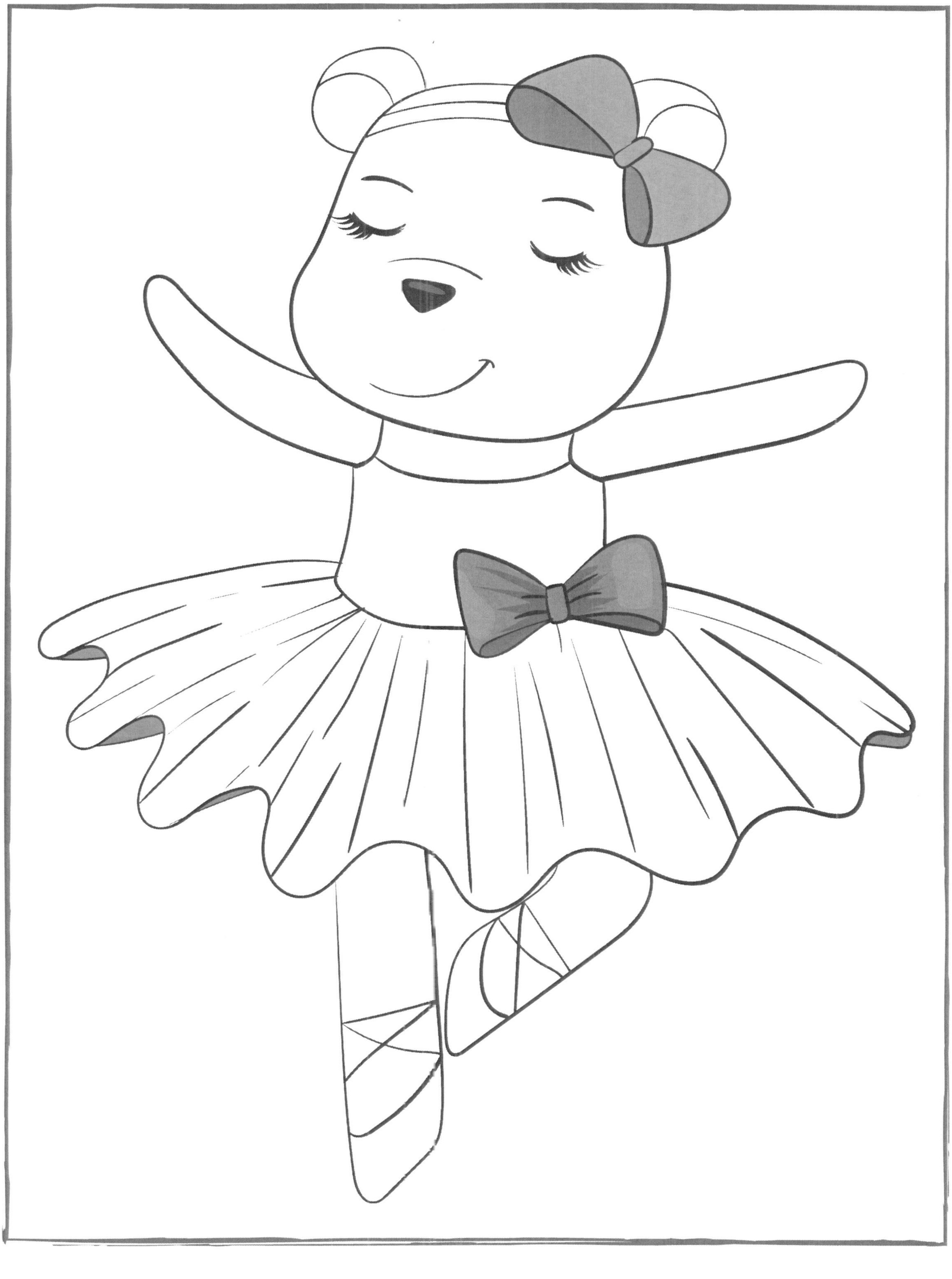

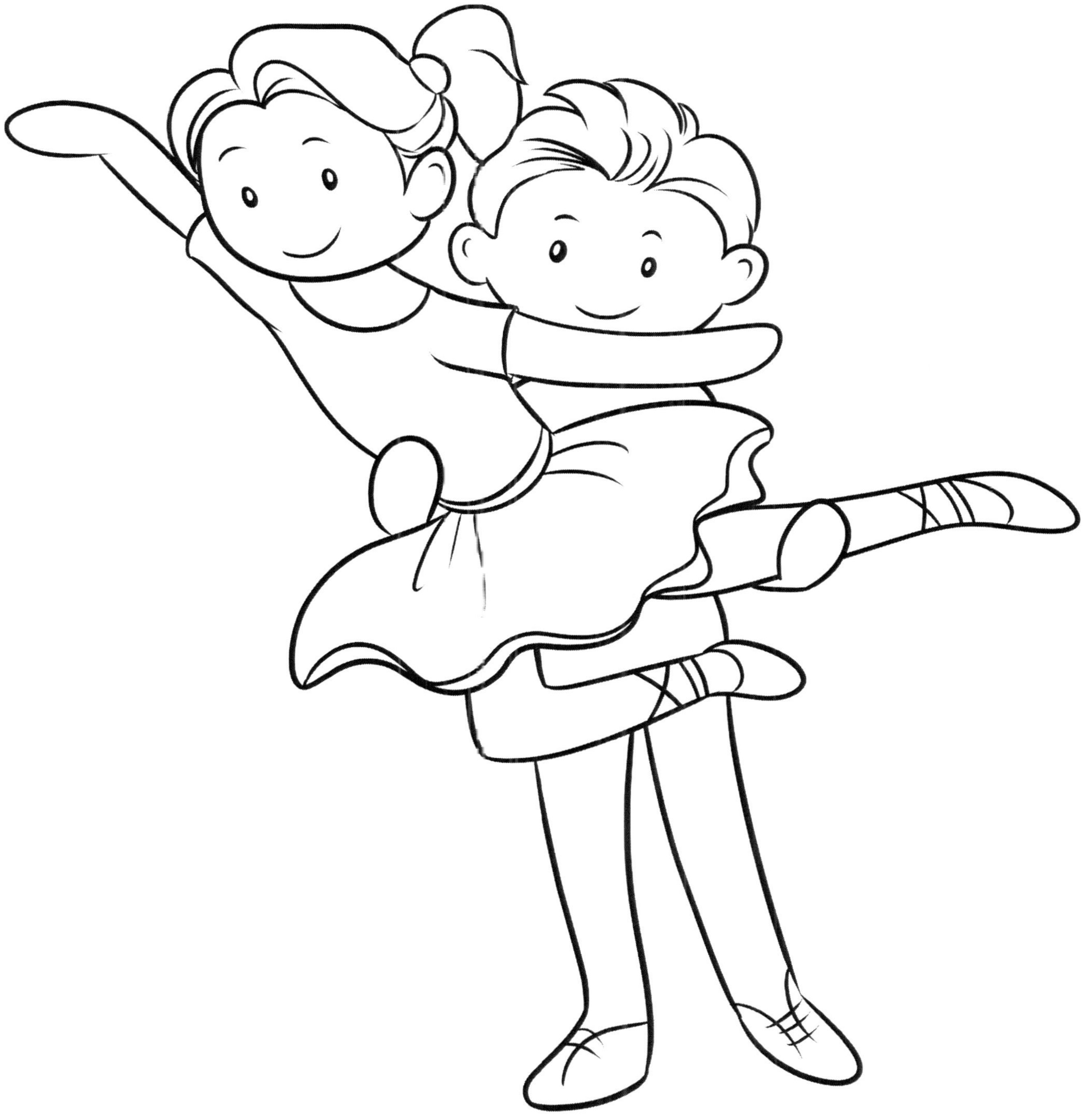

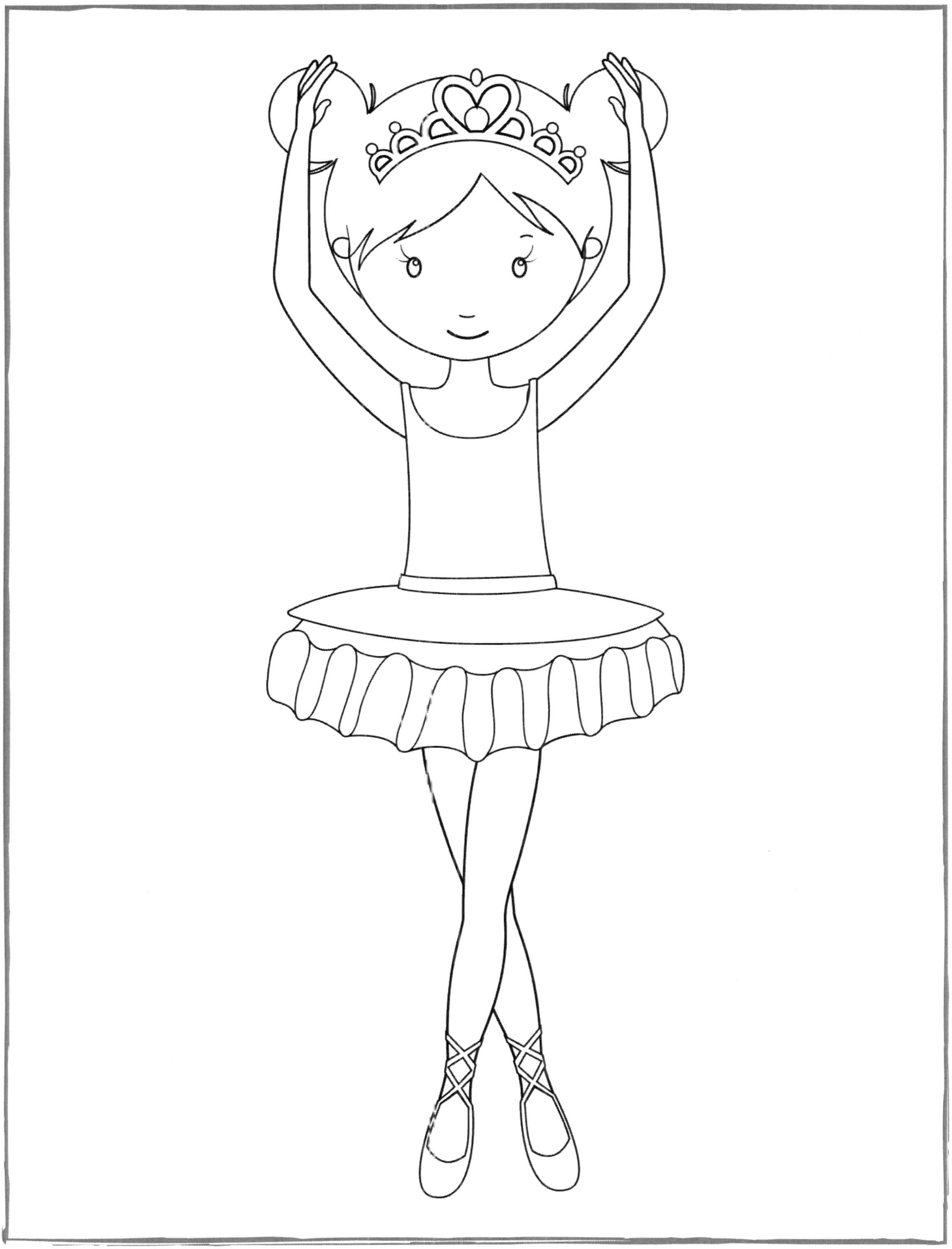

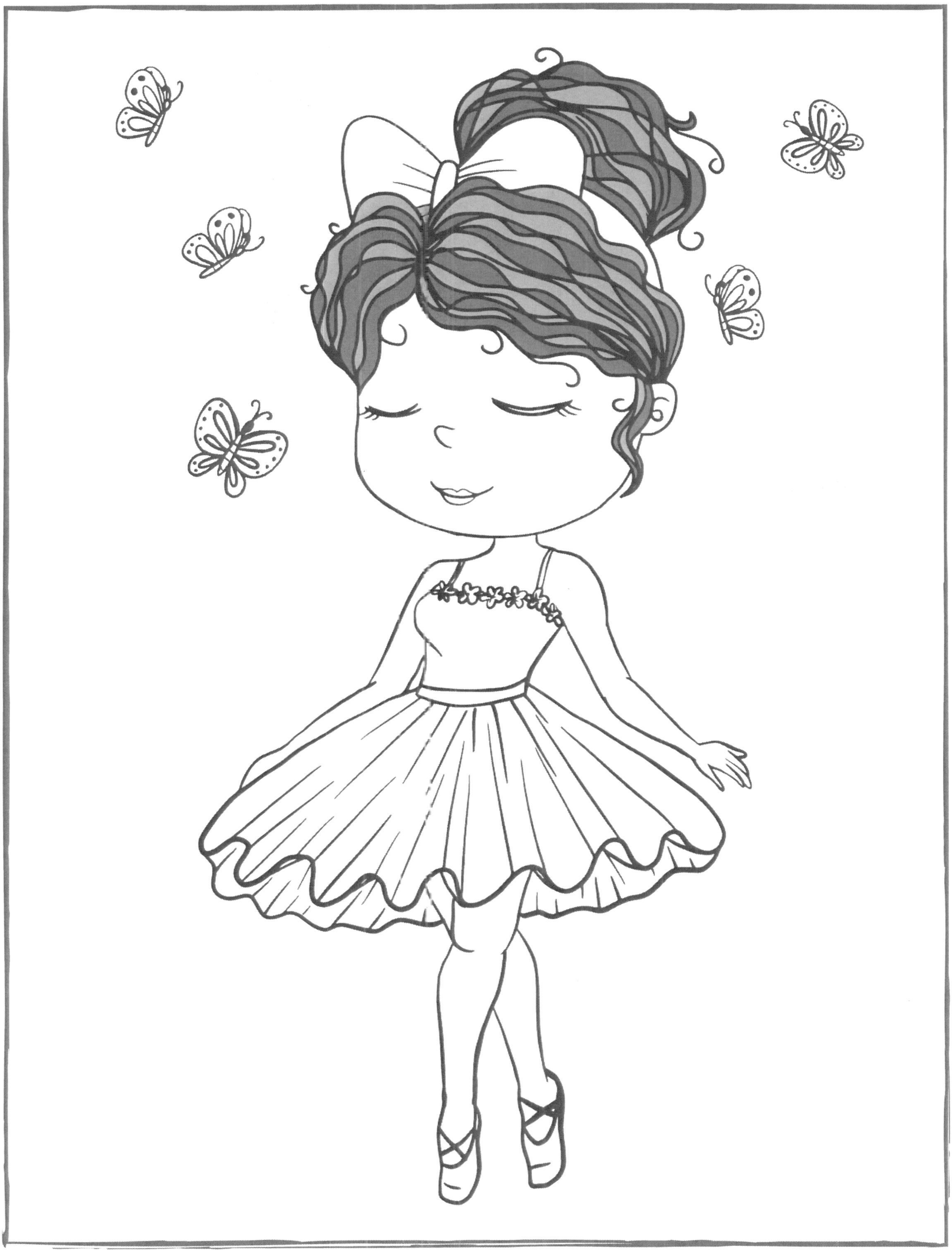

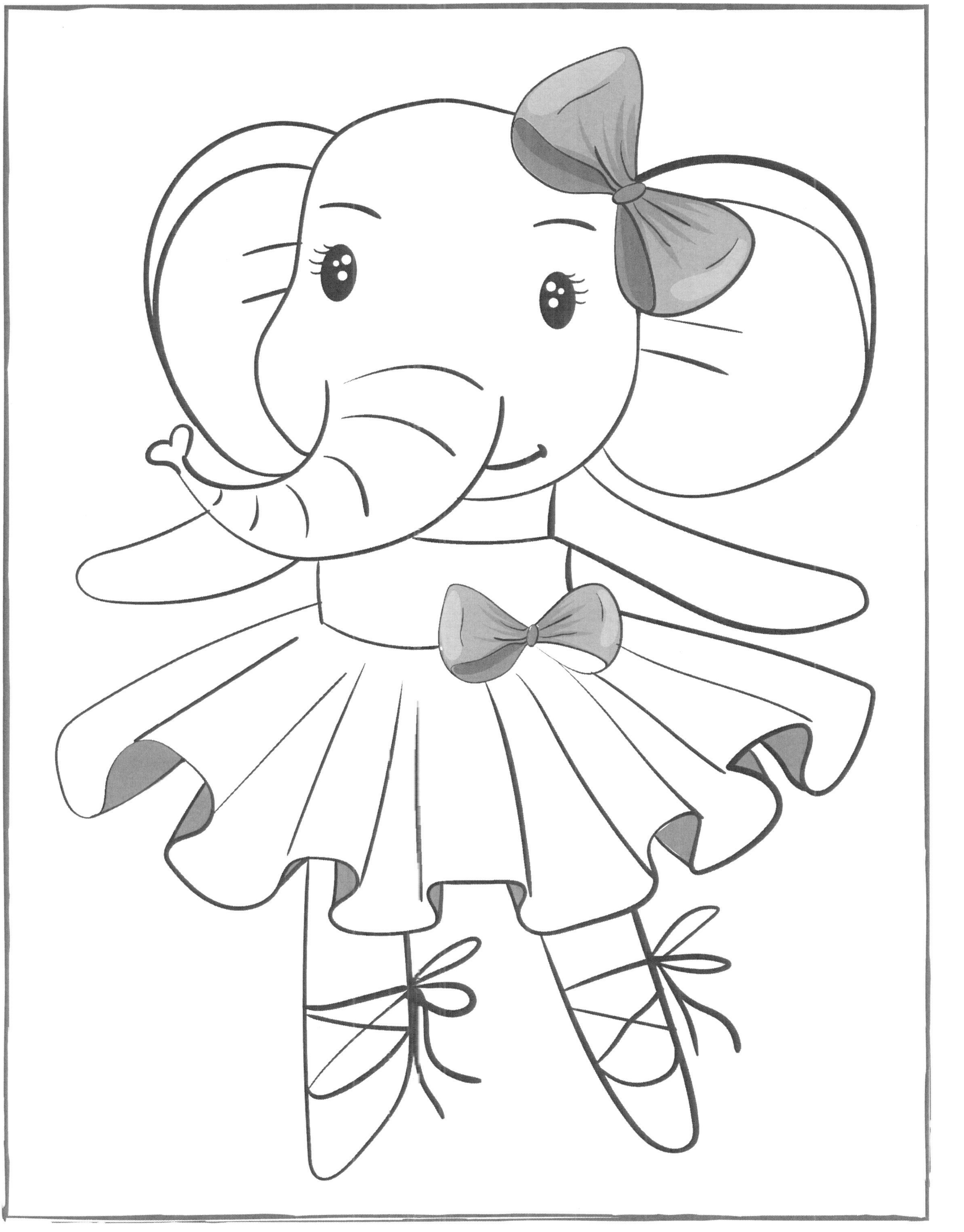

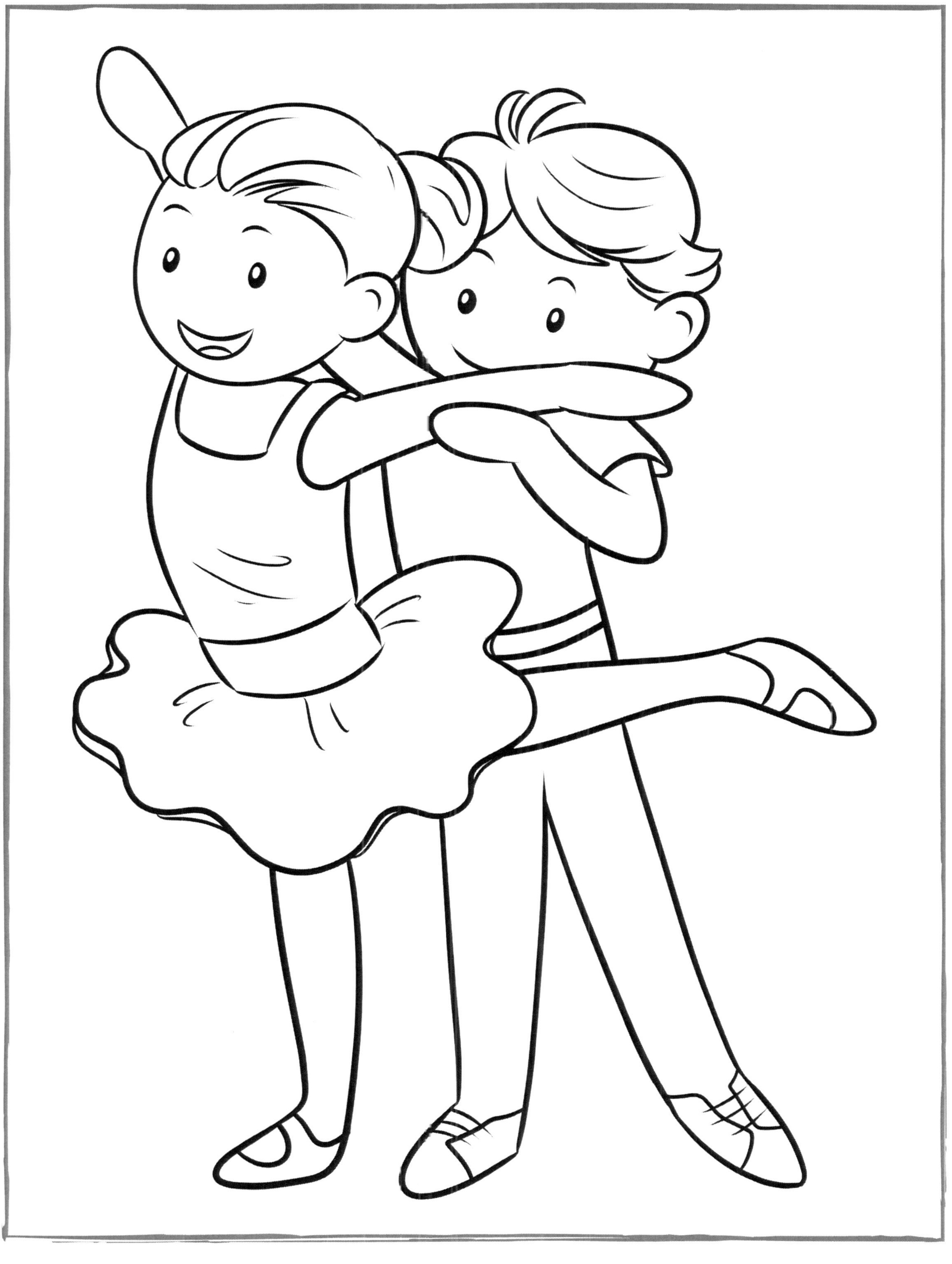

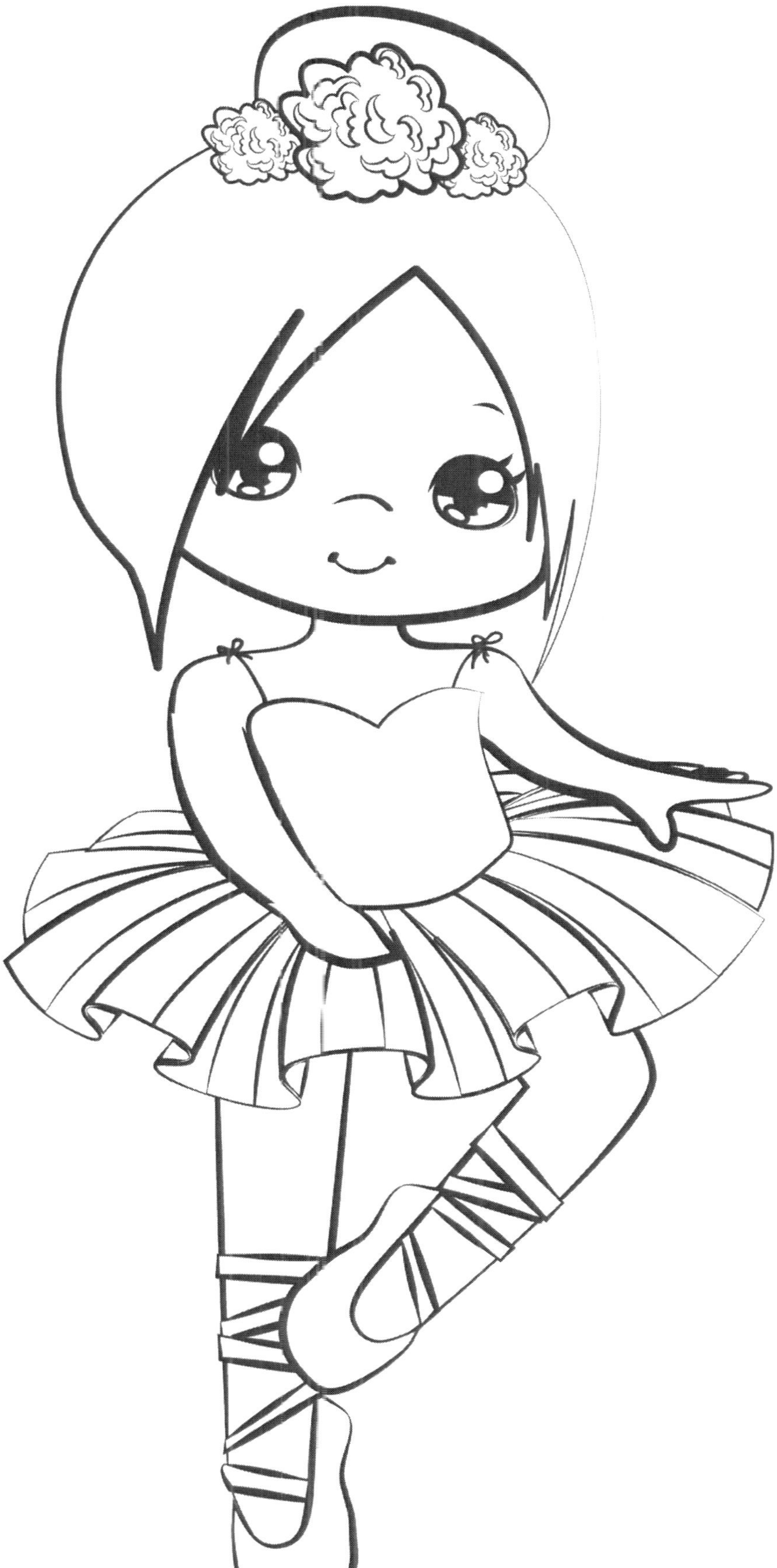

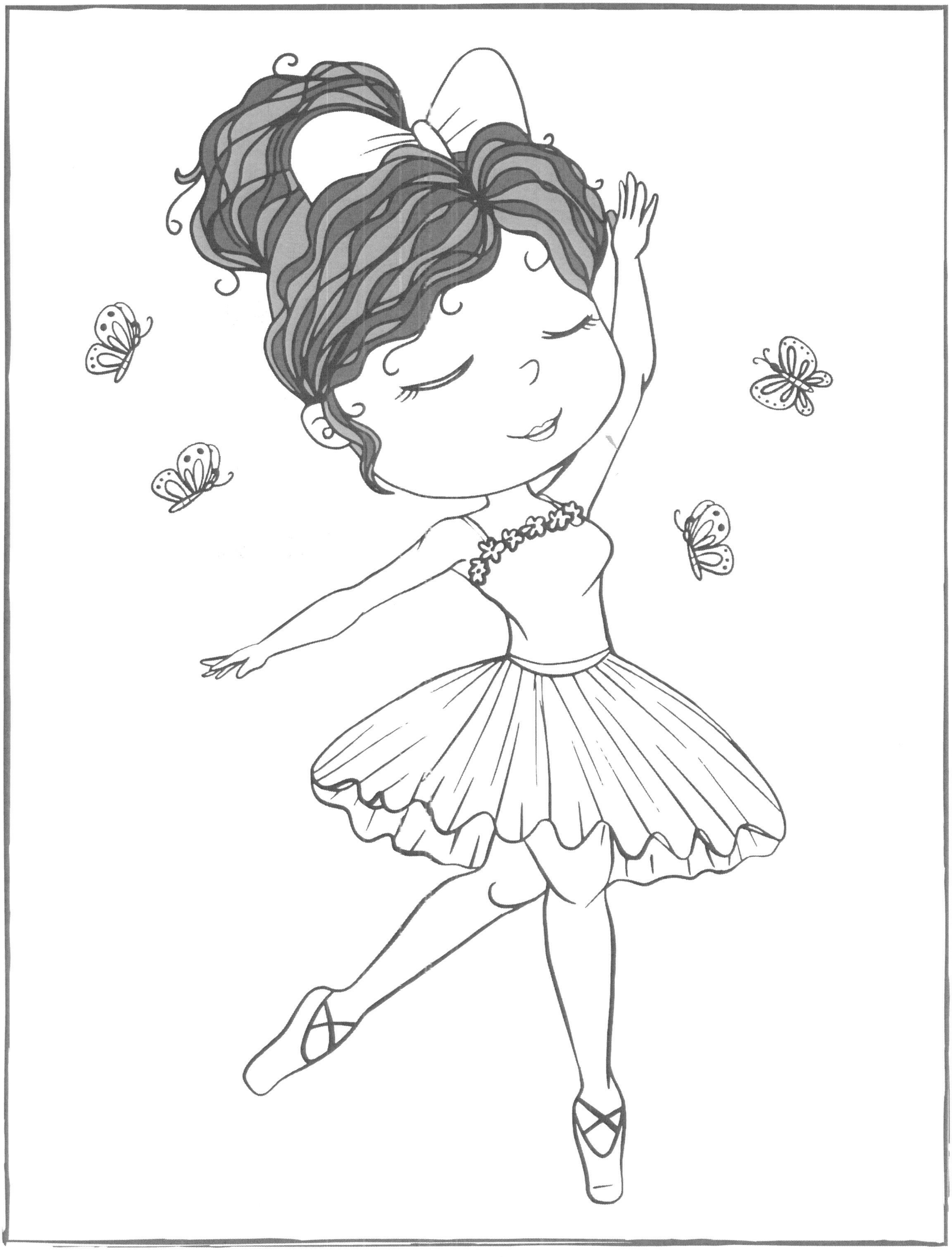

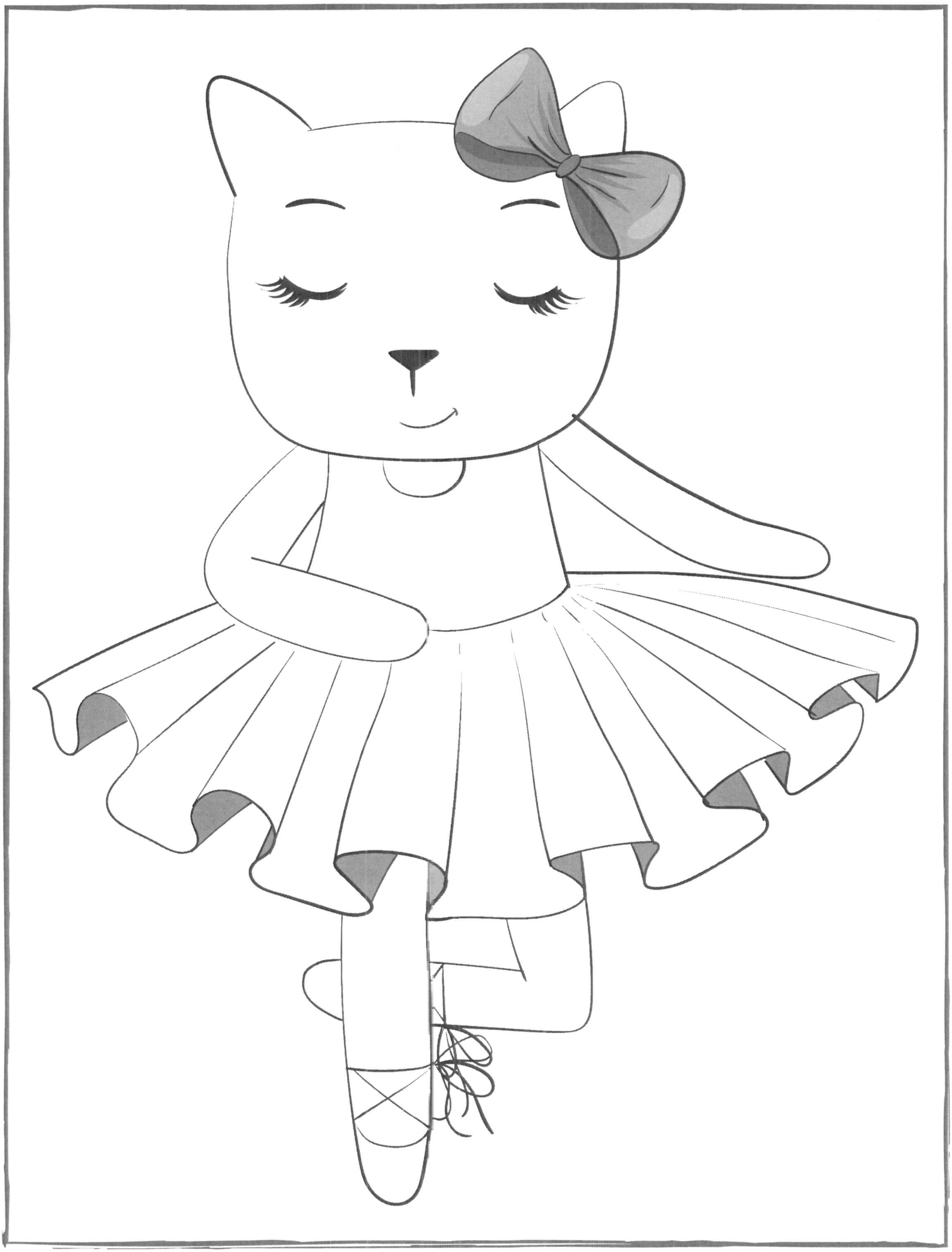

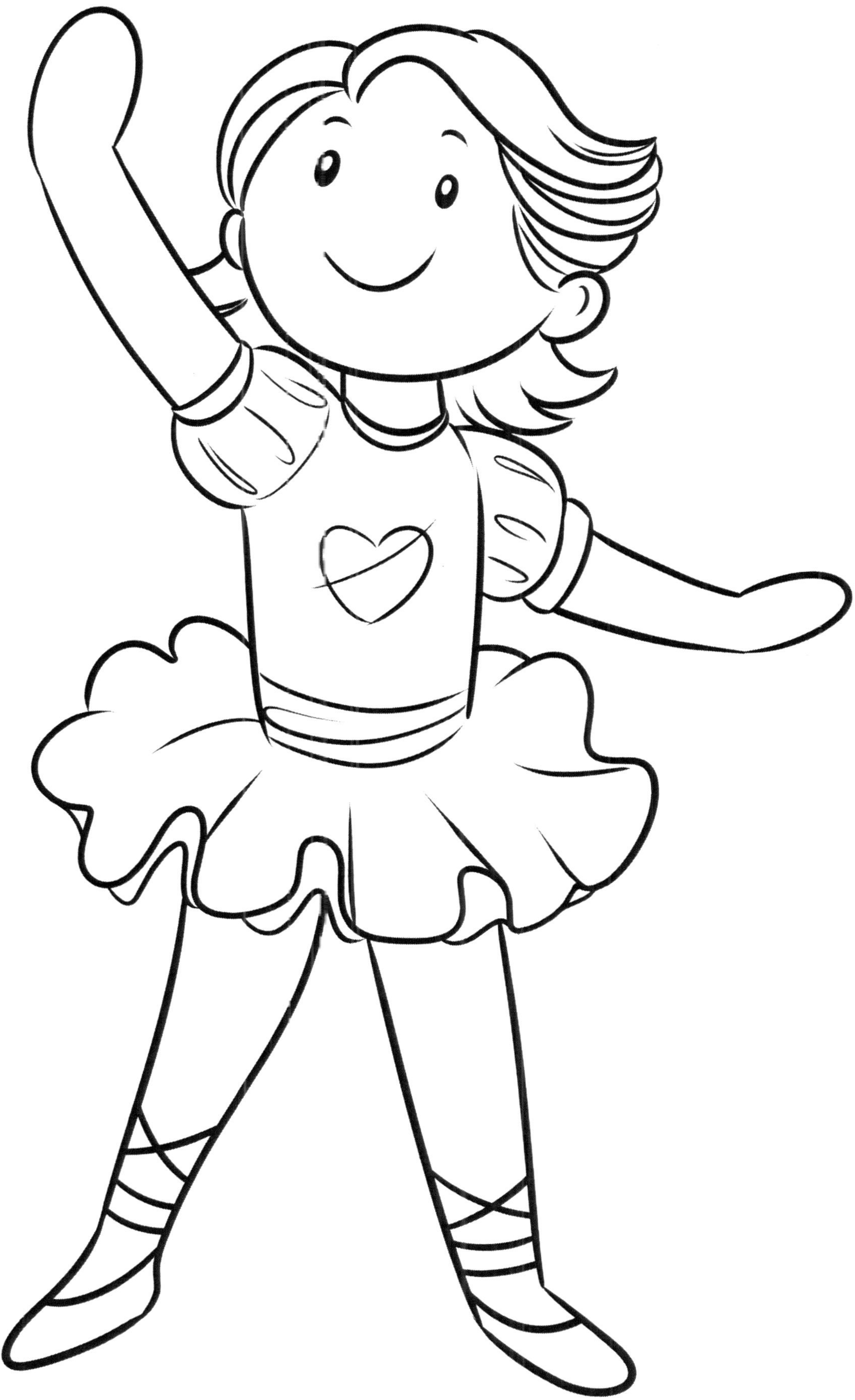

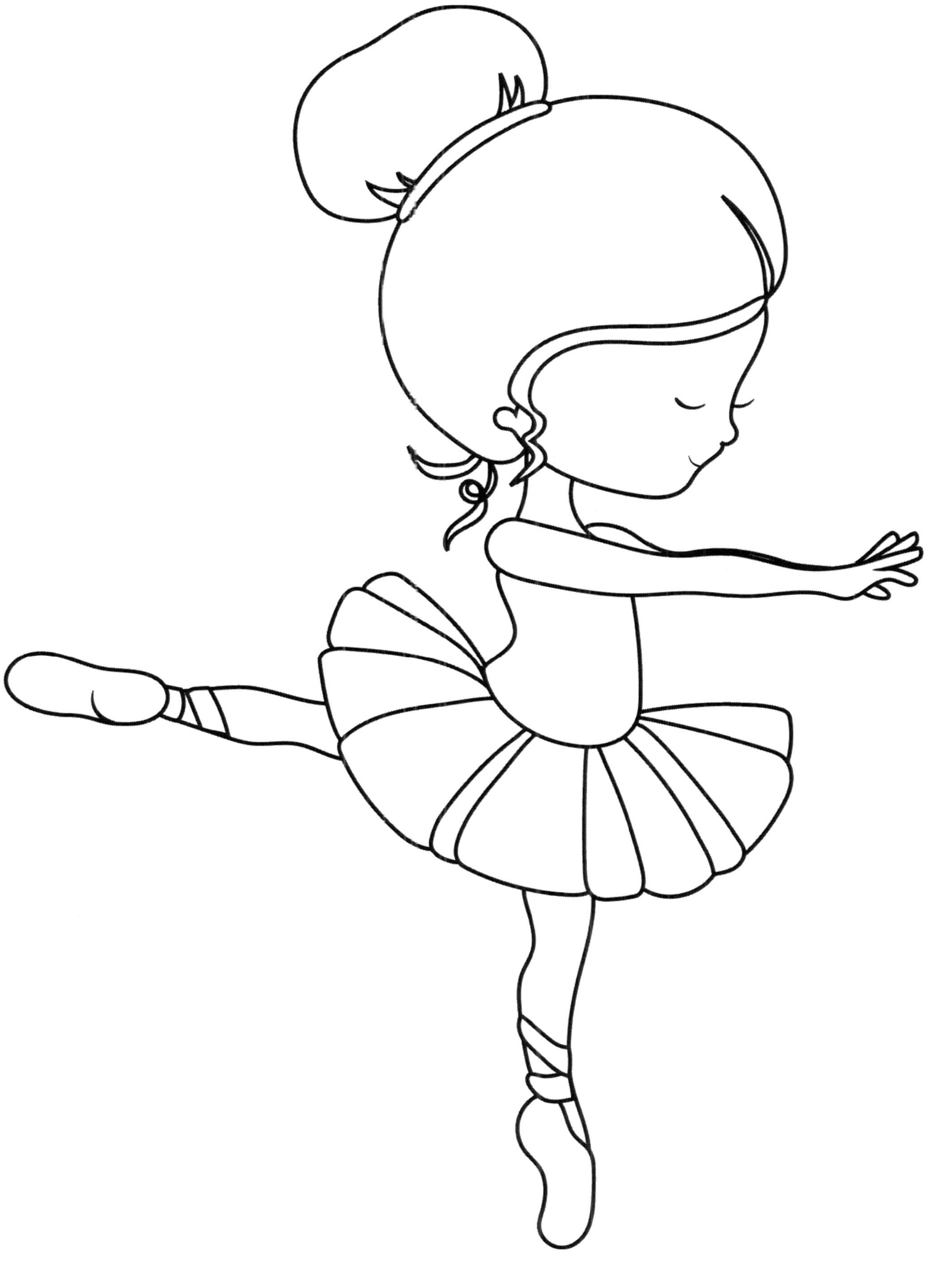

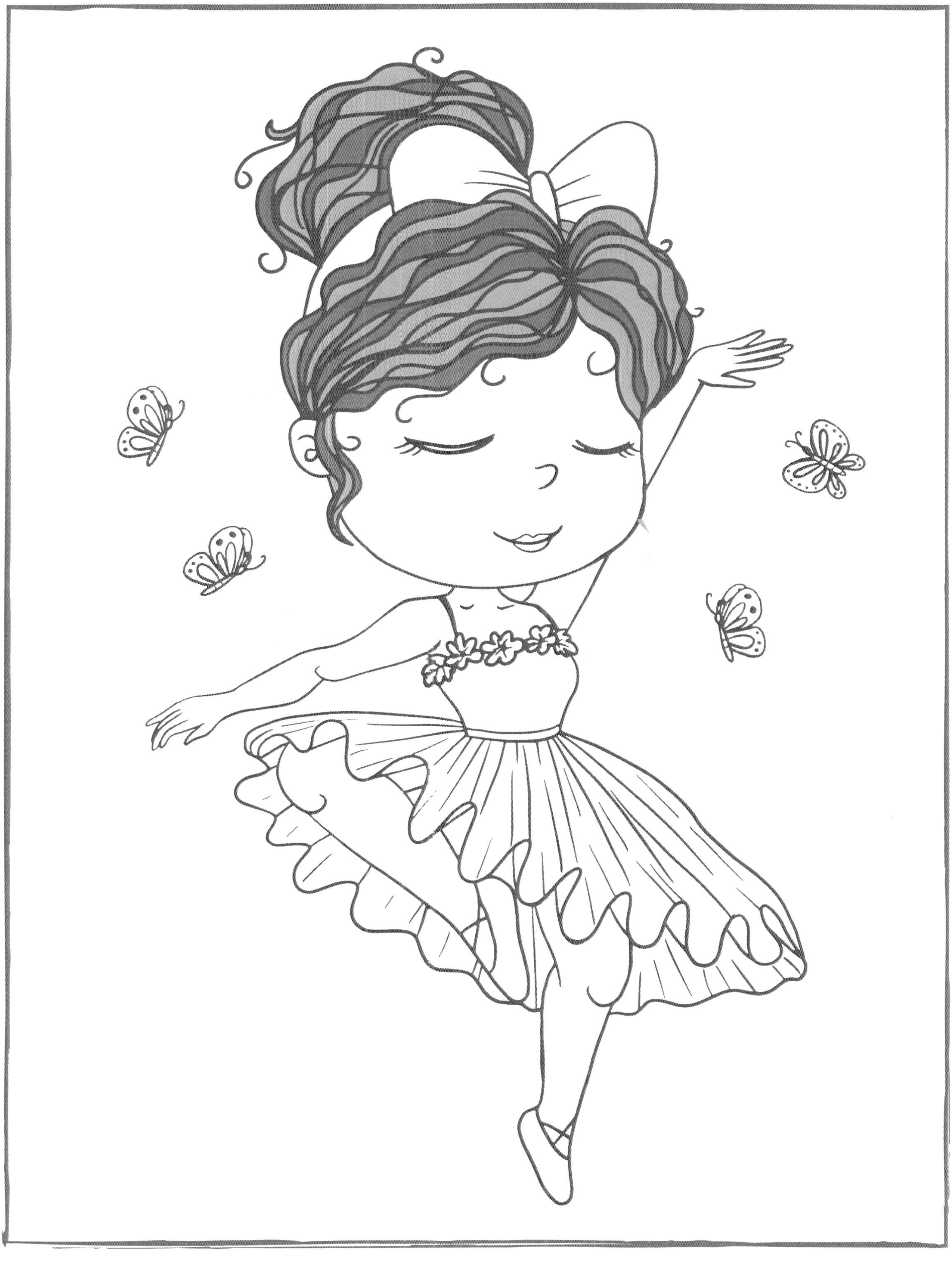

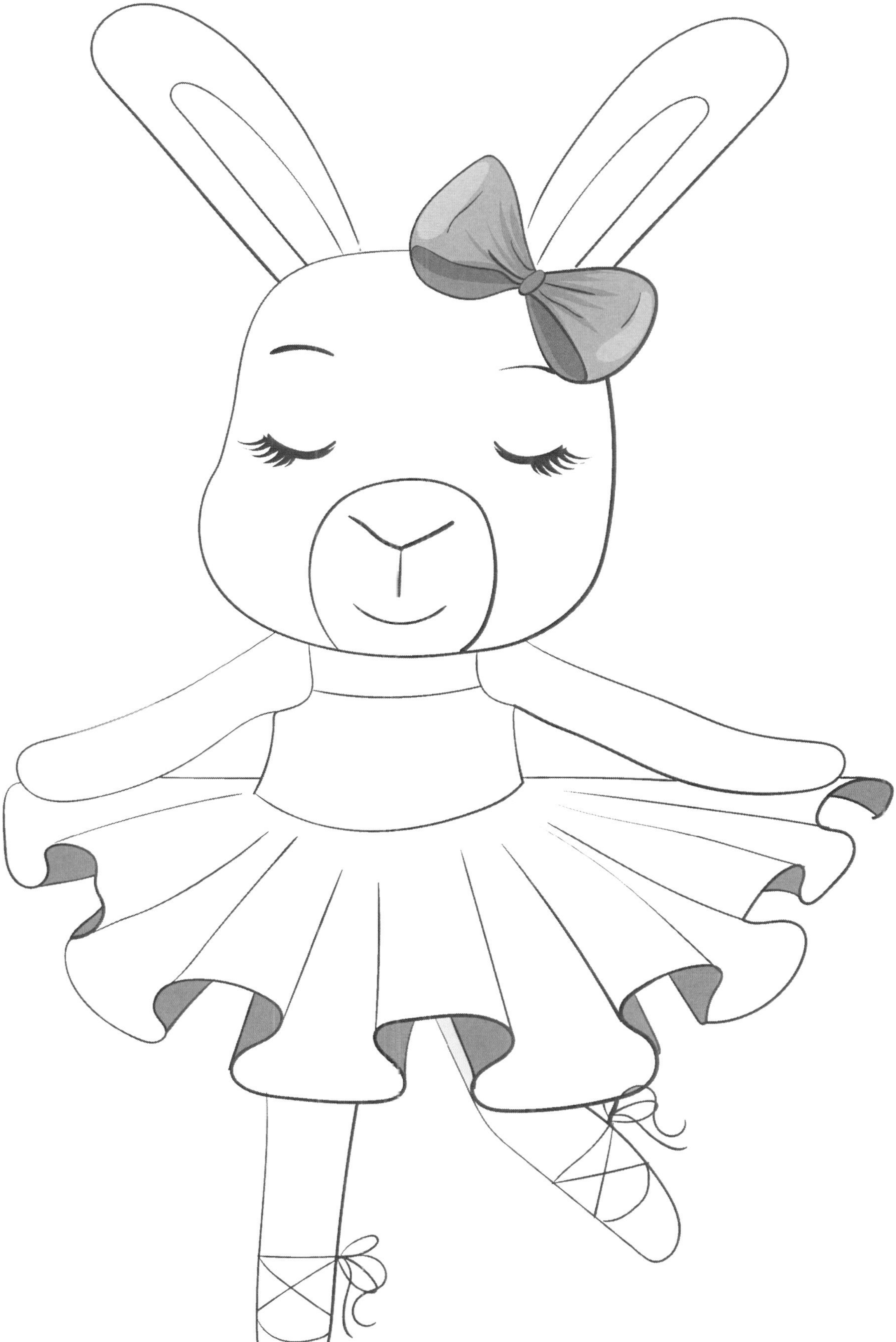

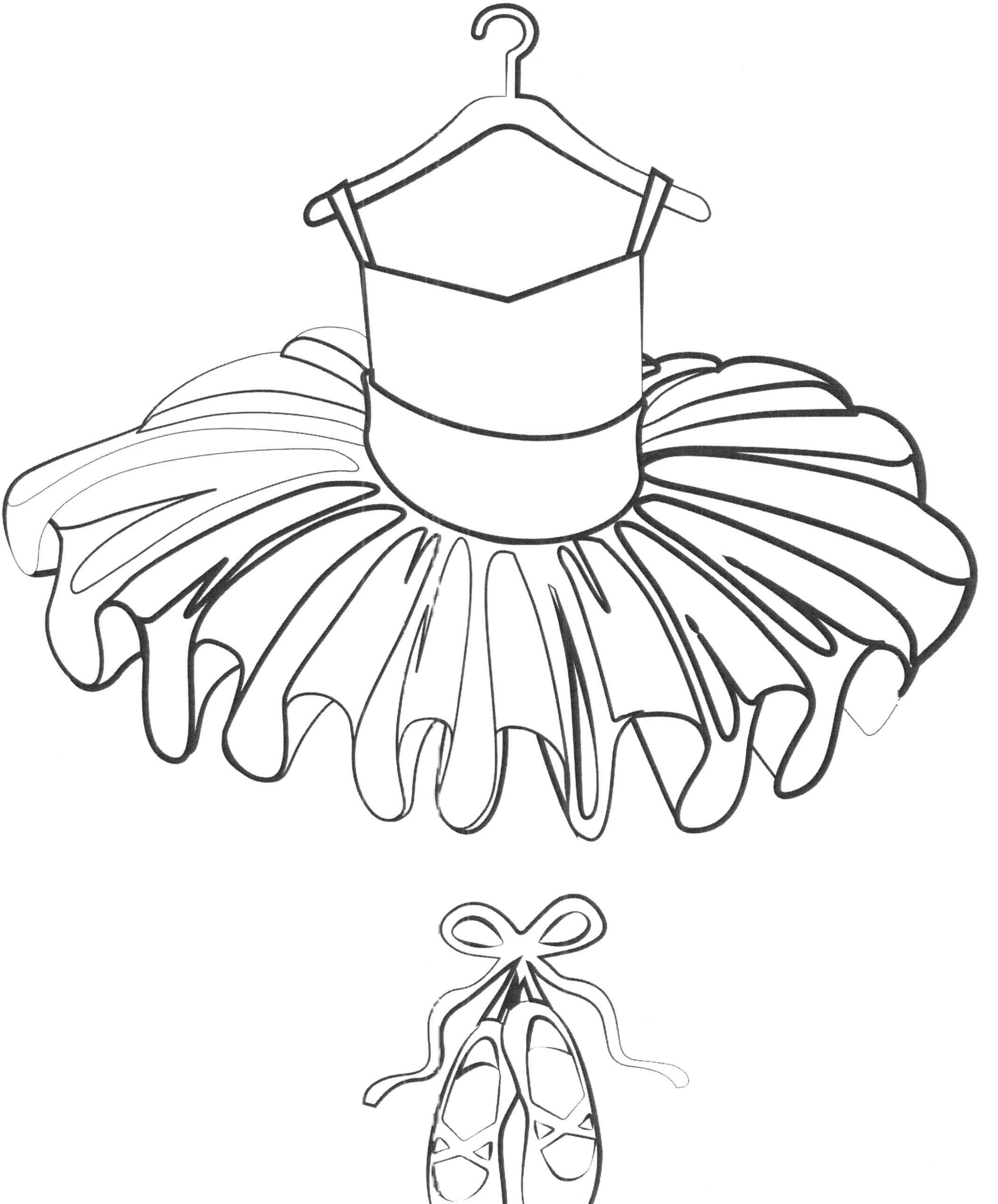

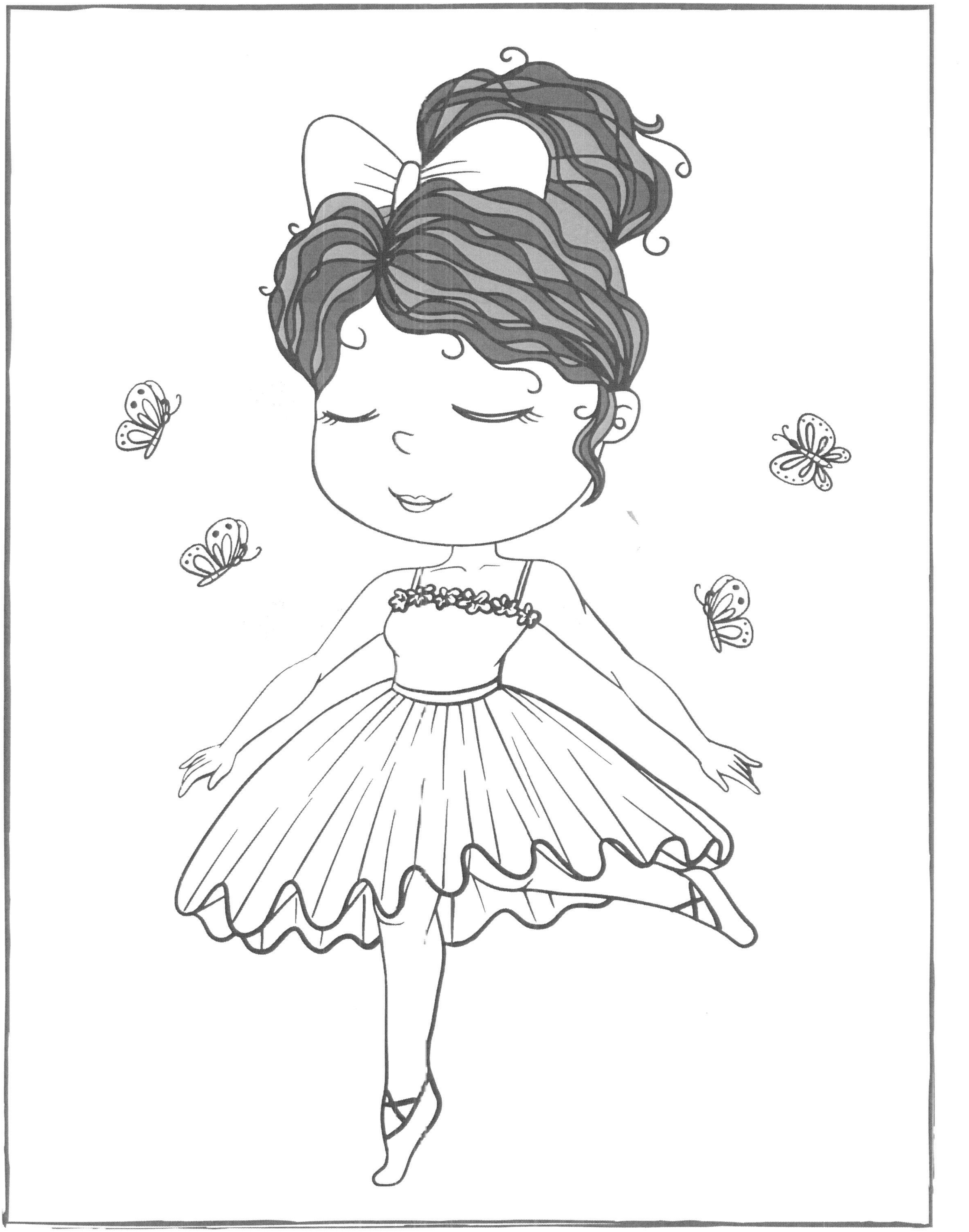

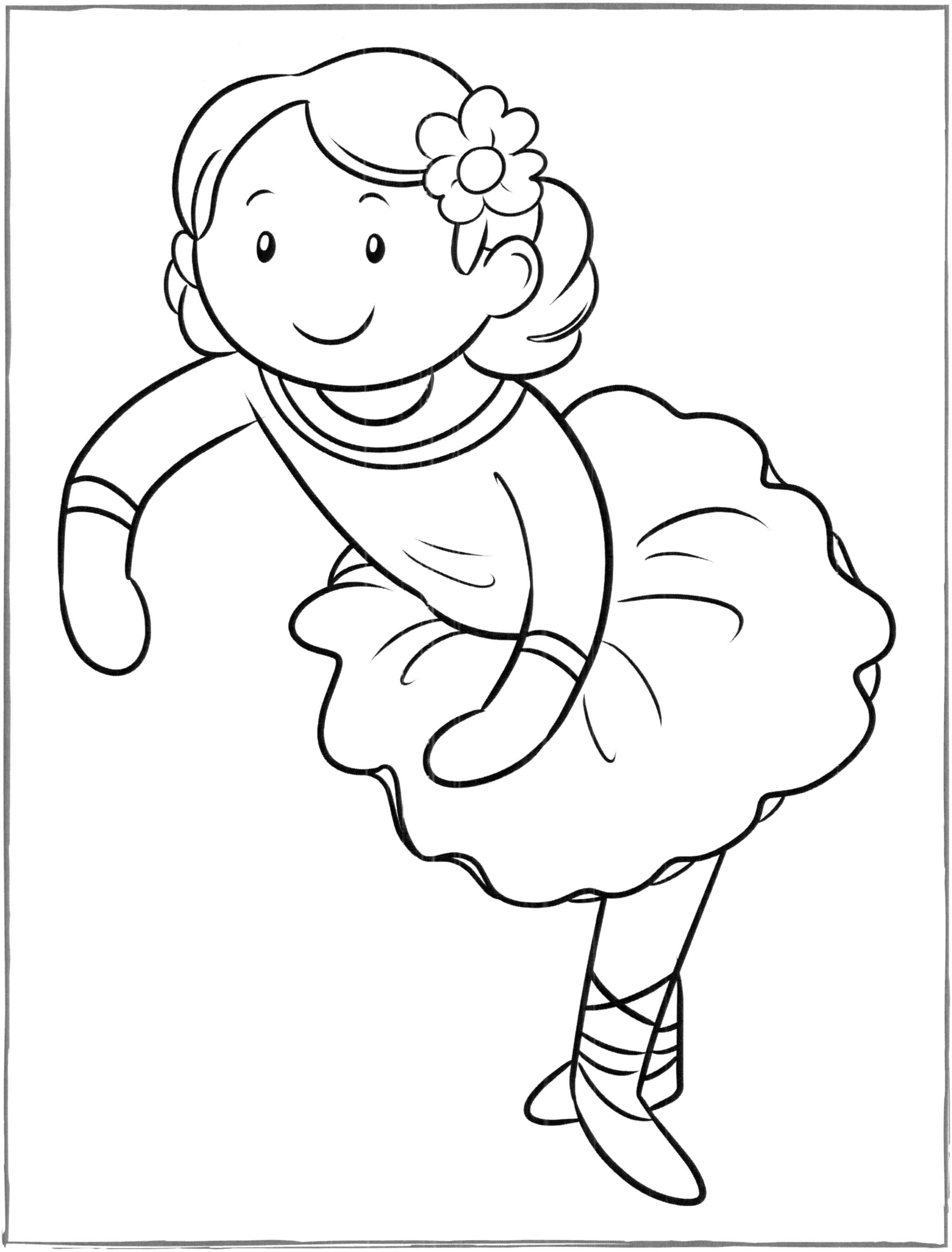

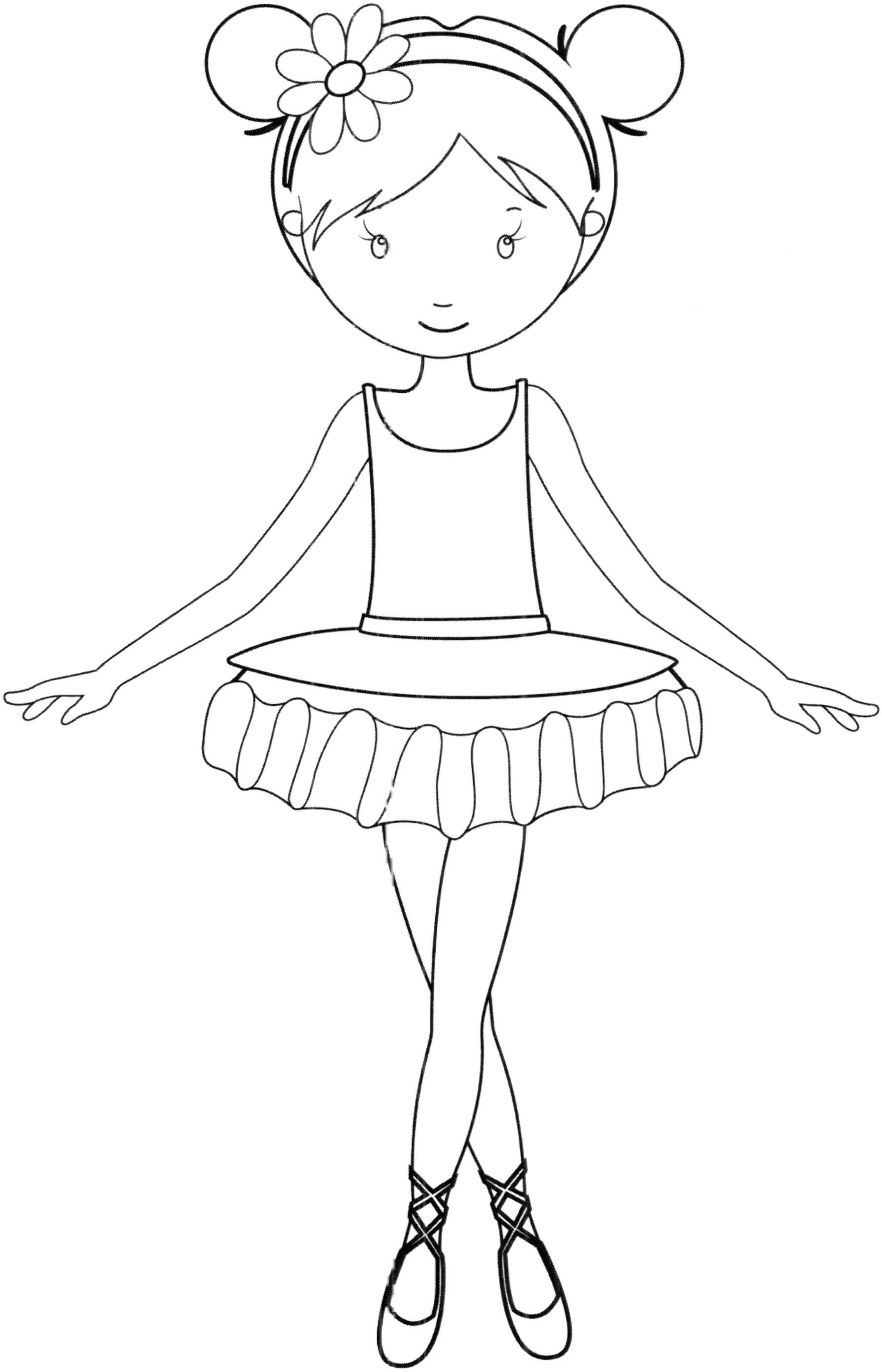

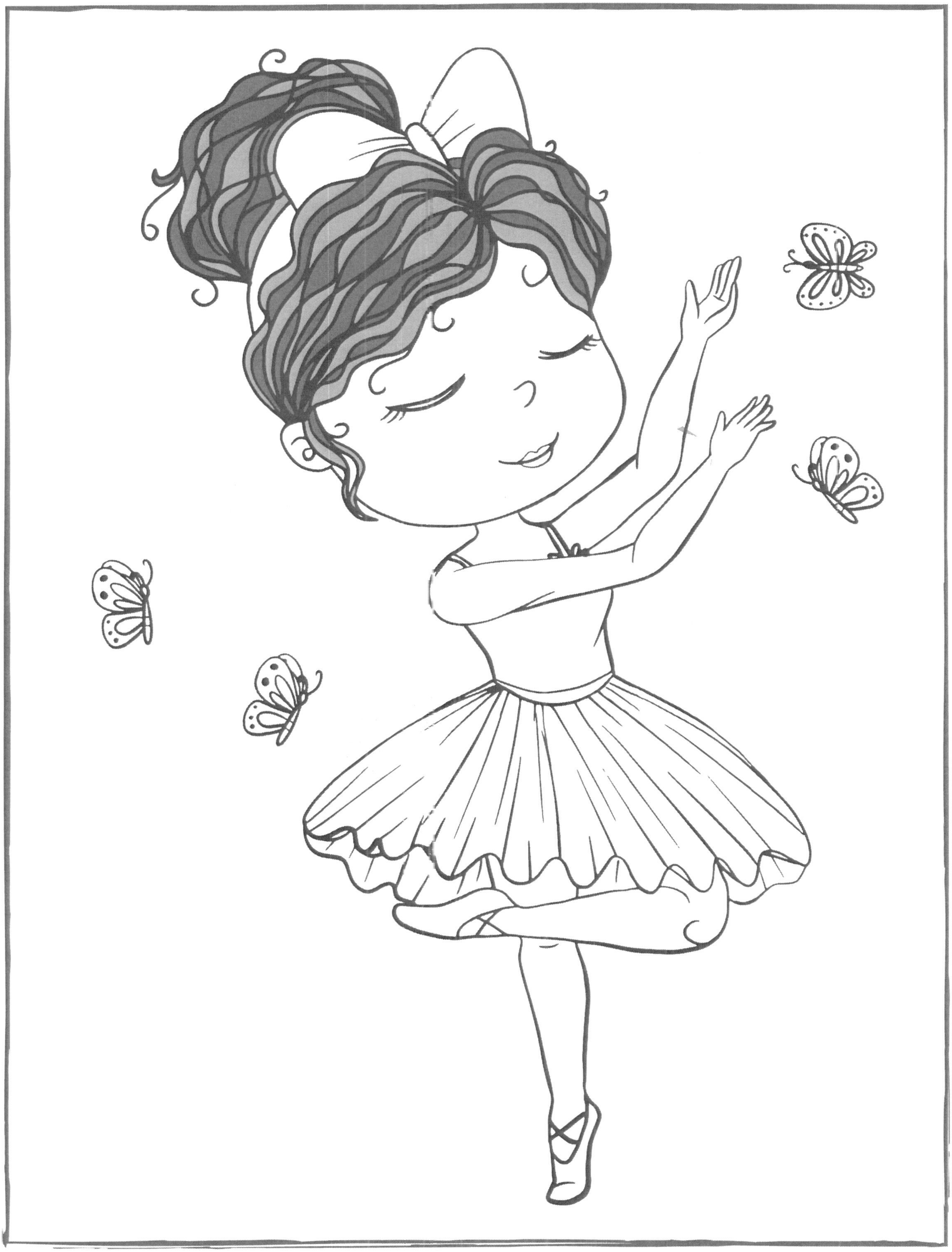

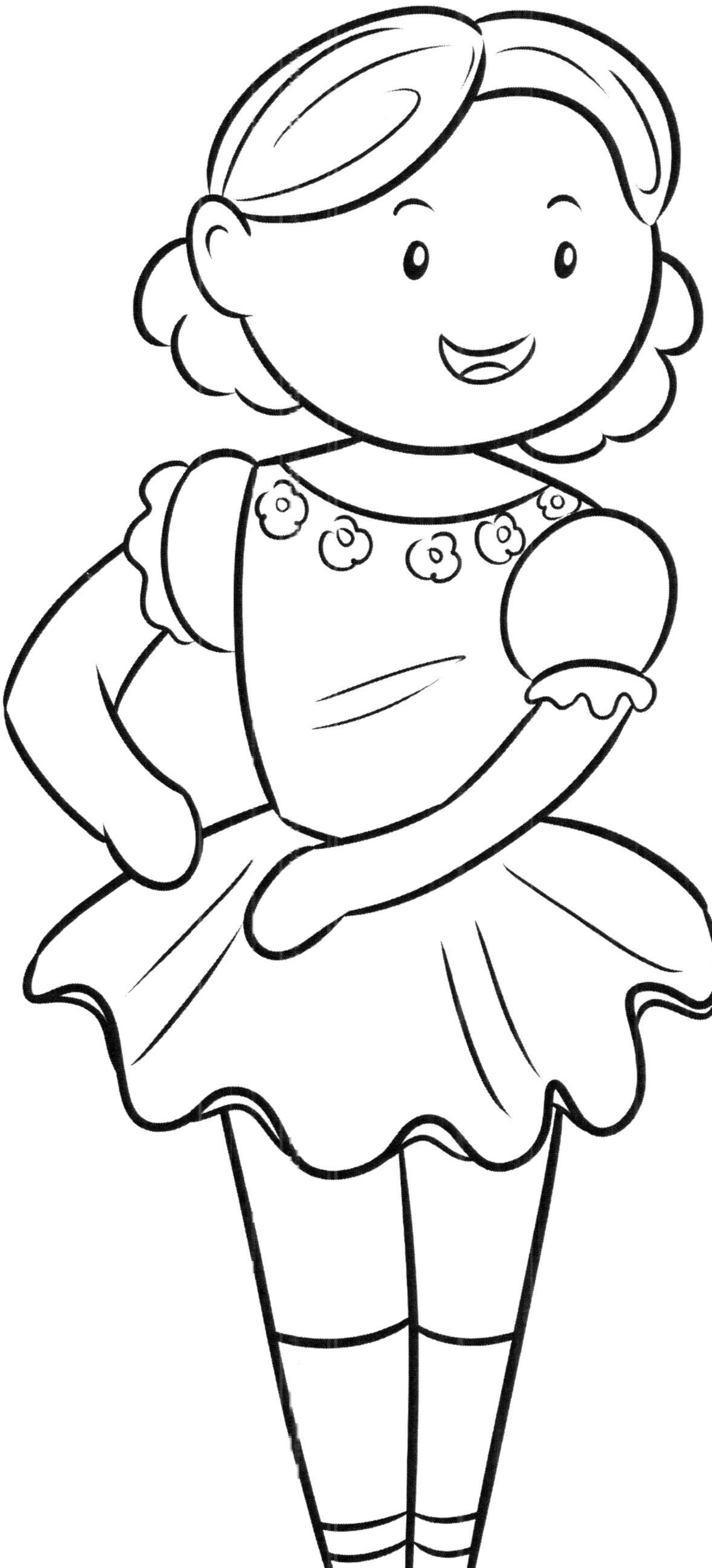

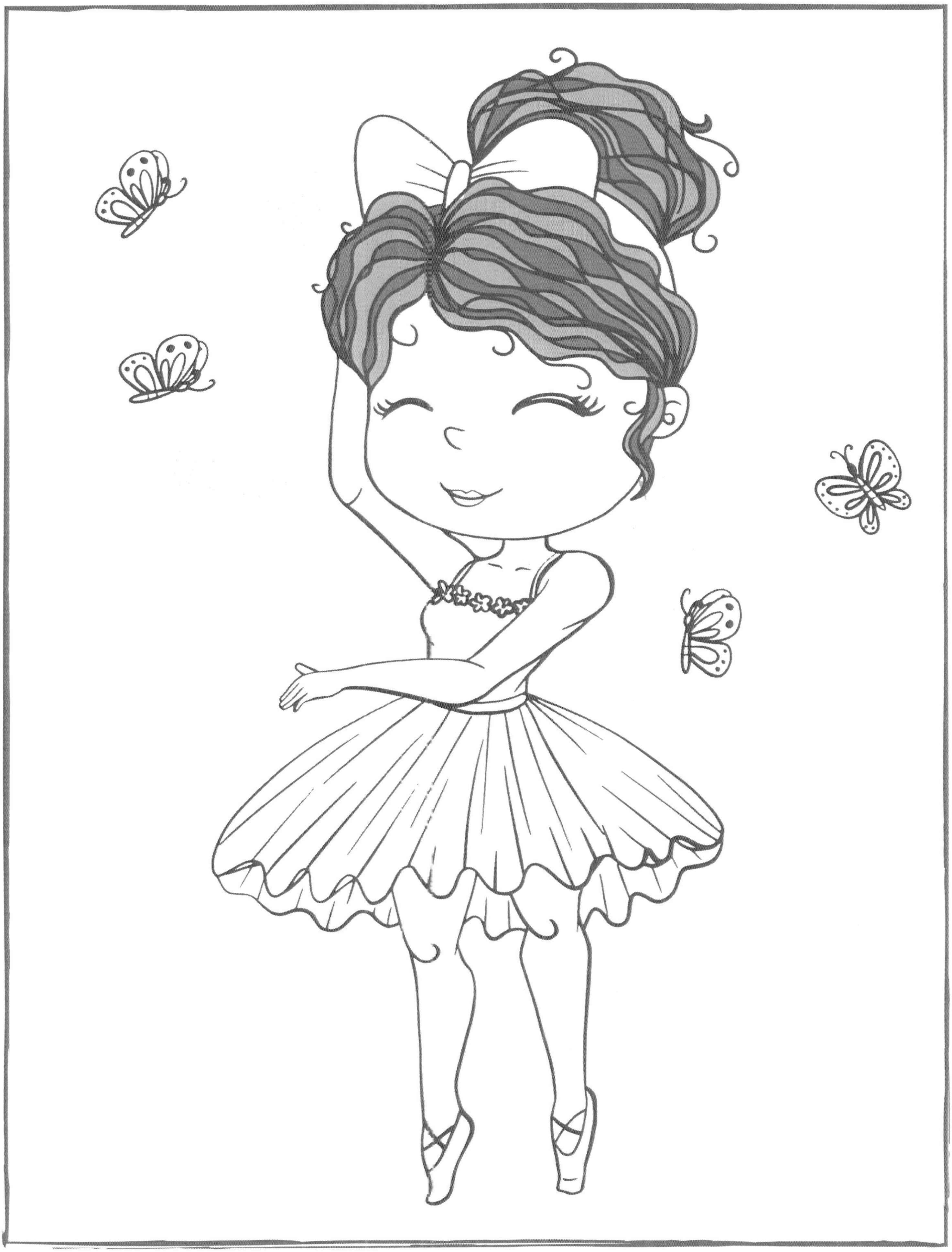

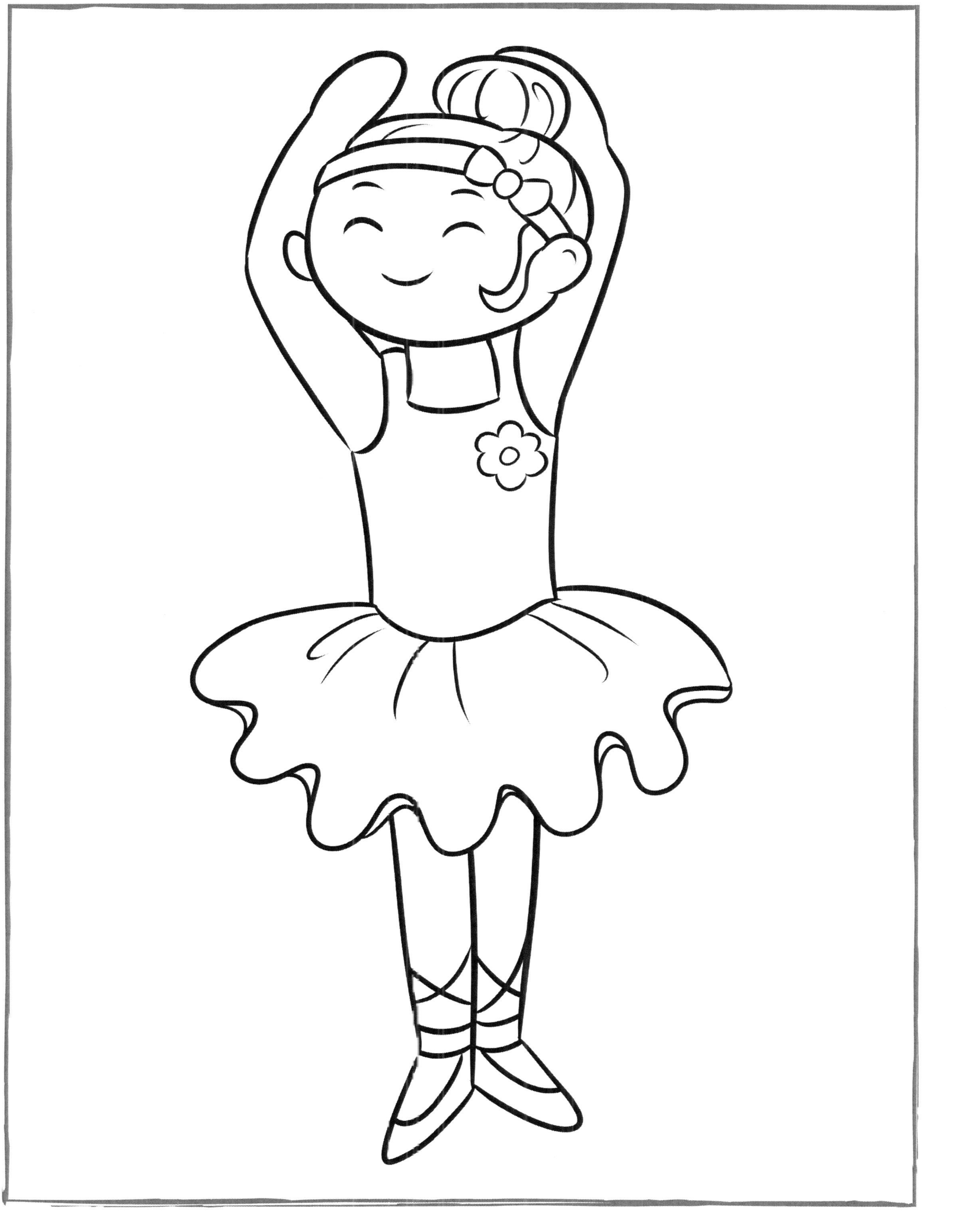

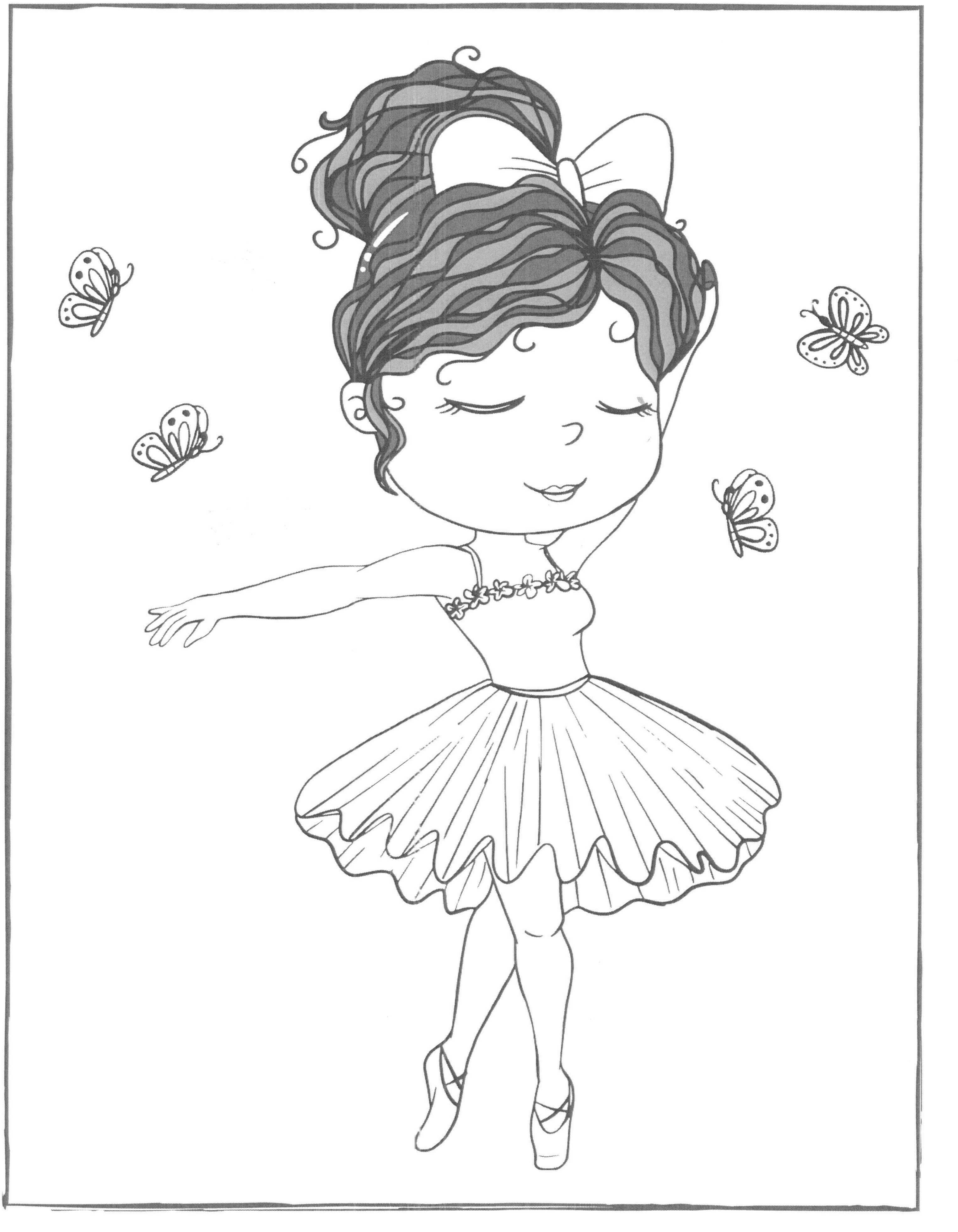

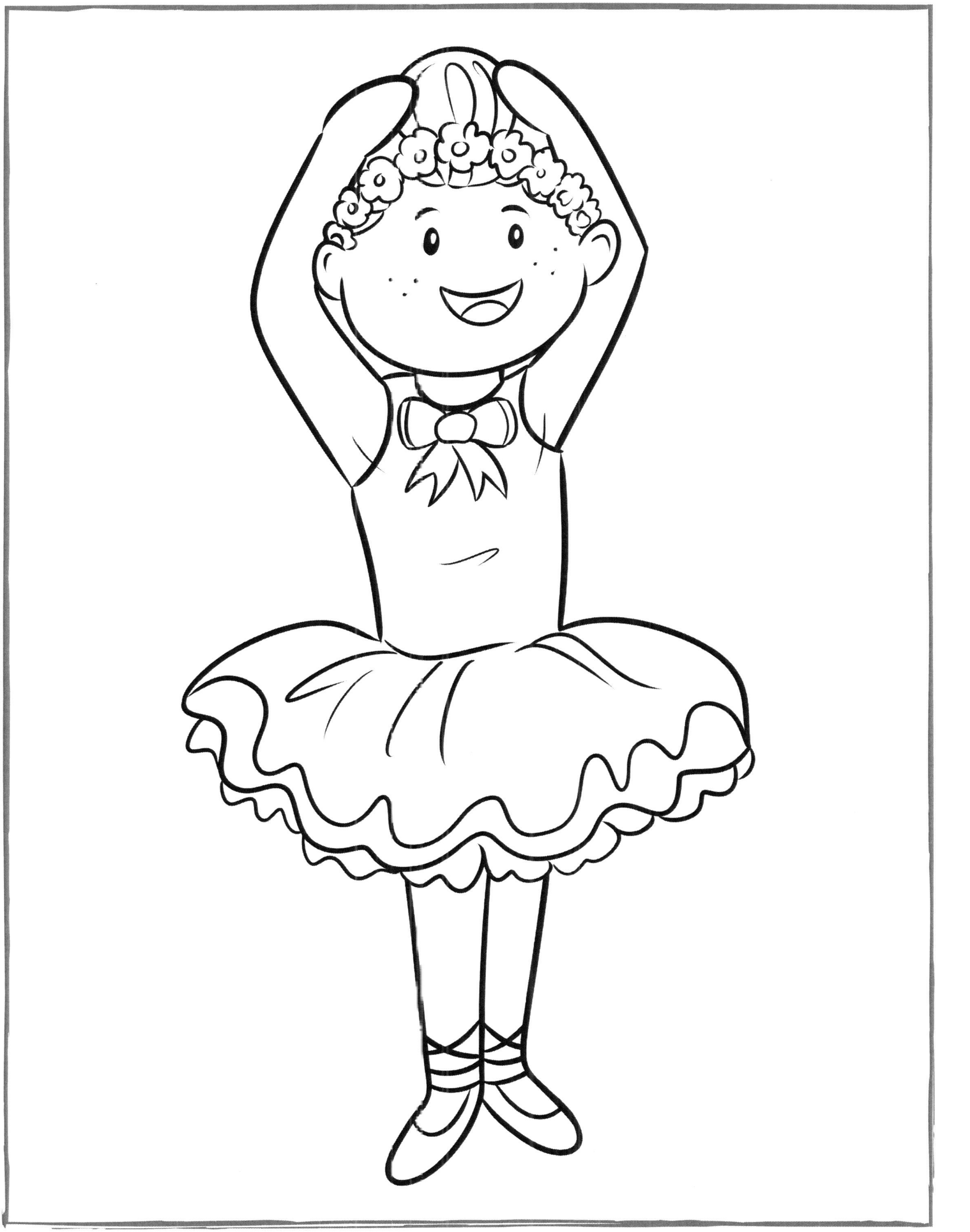

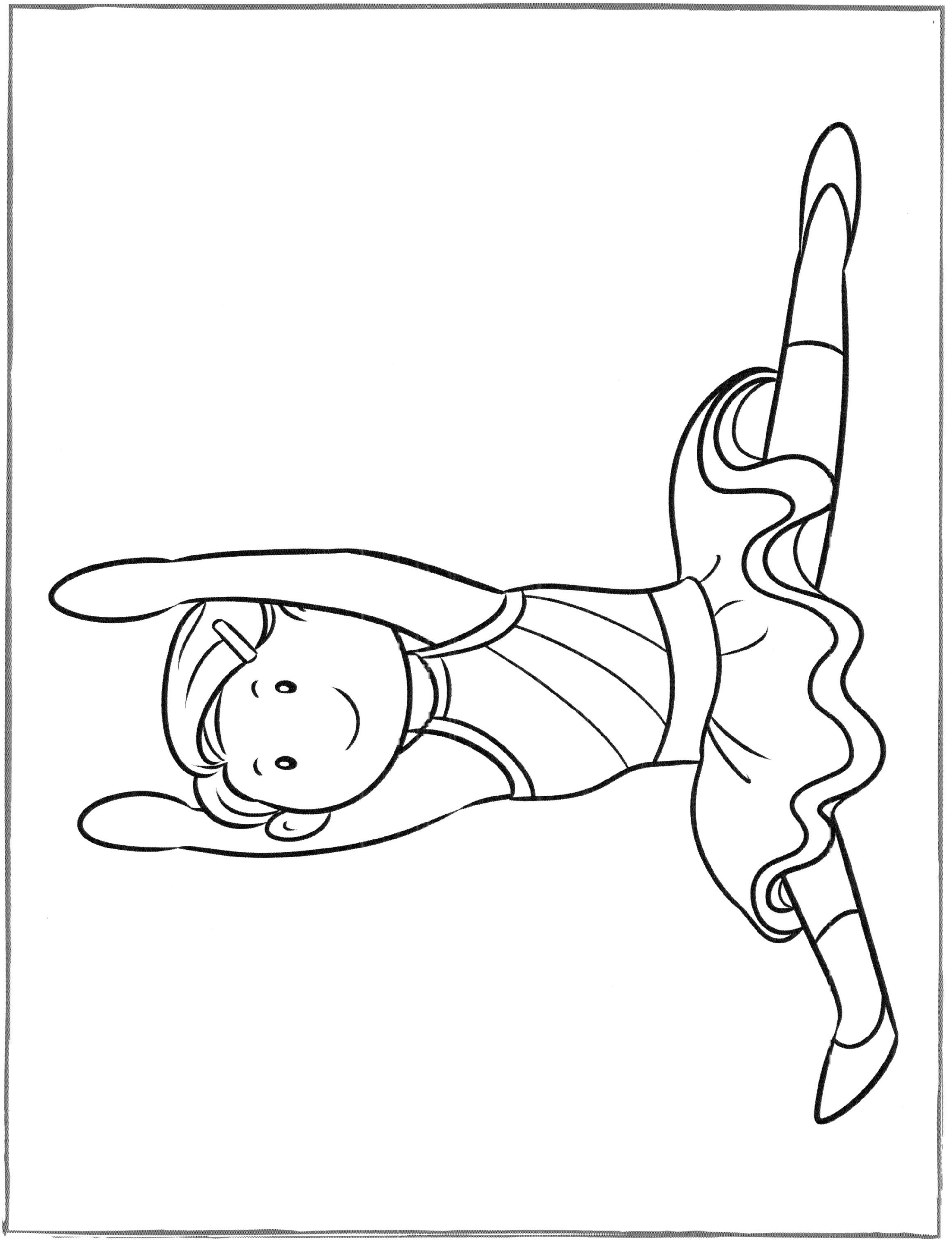

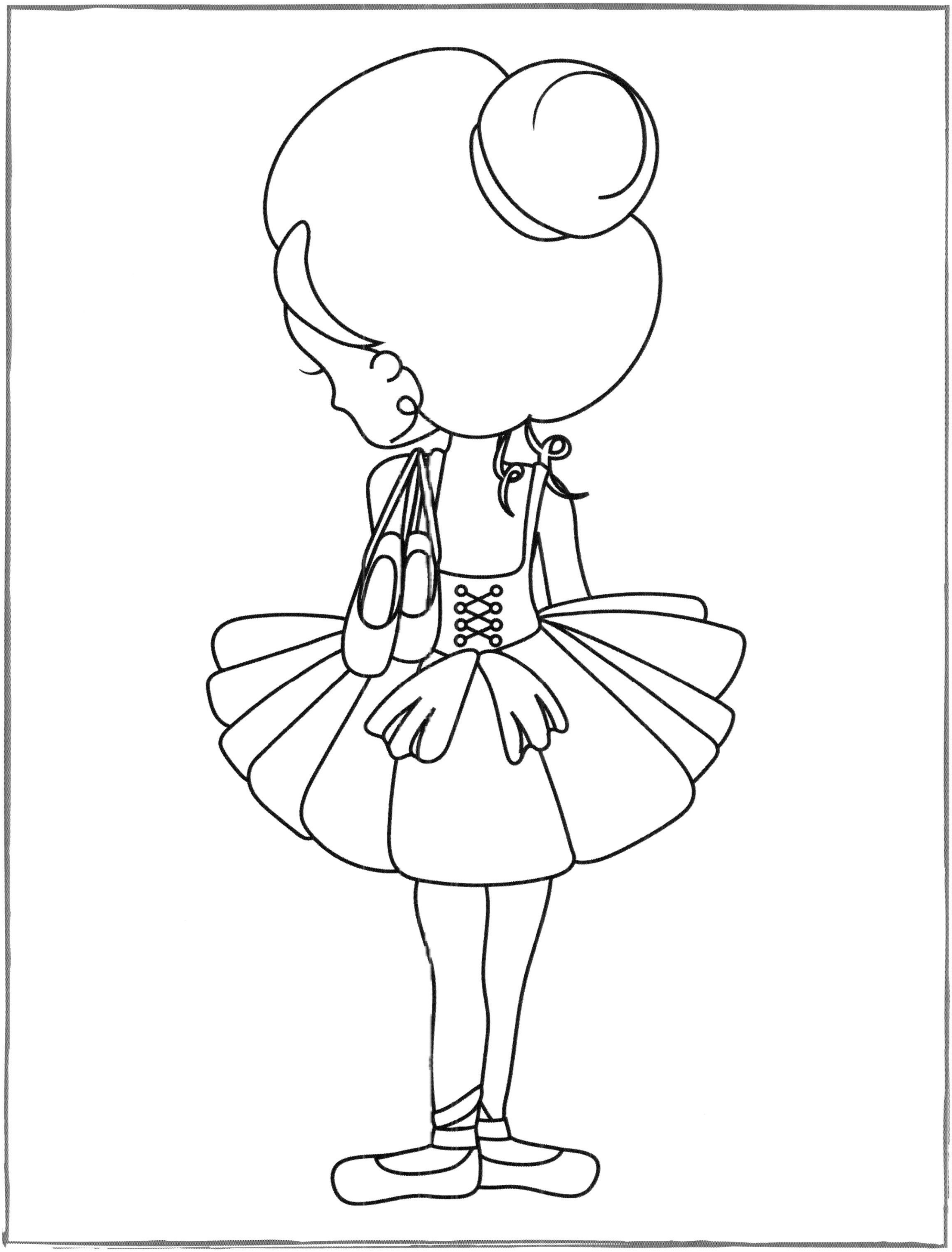

THANK YOU FOR PURCHASING THIS BOOK. WE HOPE YOU LIKED THE BOOK VERY MUCH AND WE WOULD LIKE TO ASK YOU TO ADD YOUR OPINION ON THE SELLER'S WEBSITE.

Manufactured by Amazon.ca
Acheson, AB

11244846R00037